# TAO TE CHING

# TAO TE CHING

## LAO TZU

*Introduced by*
John Baldock

*Translated by*
John H. McDonald

SIRIUS

This edition published in 2024 by Sirius Publishing, a division of
Arcturus Publishing Limited,
26/27 Bickels Yard, 151–153 Bermondsey Street,
London SE1 3HA

Designer: Sally Bond

ISBN: 978-1-3988-4079-9
AD011998UK

Printed in China

# CONTENTS

# INTRODUCTION

The *Tao Te Ching* is not only the most influential classic text of Chinese philosophy, it is also one of the most widely read examples of what can perhaps best be described as 'wisdom literature'.

According to tradition, the *Tao Te Ching* was written in the 6th century BCE by the Taoist sage Lao Tzu, a contemporary of Confucius (K'ung Fu-tzu, 551–479 BCE). However, analysis of the text's vocabulary and style suggests a date some time in the late 4th or early 3rd century BCE. Several ancient versions of the Chinese text exist, but the oldest extant version was discovered in 1993 in a tomb near the town of Guodian in Hubei Province. Written on numerous slips of bamboo, a common writing material in ancient China, this text has been dated prior to 300 BCE. Initially the text was known simply as the Lao Tzu, but during the Han period (1st century BCE to 1st century CE) it became more widely known under its present name of the *Tao Te Ching* – a title that derives from the traditional division of the book's 81 short chapters into two sections. The first section (Chapters 1 to 37) opens with an explanation of the enigmatic nature of the *Tao* (literally, 'the Way'), while the second (Chapters 38 to 81) opens with an explanation of the workings of *Te* (virtue, power, quality, or 'the good'). The third word, namely *Ching*, means 'classic', and so *Tao Te Ching* can be translated as 'The Classic of the Way and Its Power (or Virtue)'.

Although the *Tao Te Ching* is of primary importance for the Taoist school of Chinese philosophy as well as the Taoist religion and Chinese Buddhism, its translation into hundreds of languages has made it available to a world-wide audience. The original text comprised around 5,000 Chinese characters, some of which have multiple meanings; it was also written in a cryptic style. If we add to this the differences between Chinese and Western thought and the passage of time between the writing of the original text and the present day, we can begin to appreciate the difficulties faced by translators in their efforts to provide an effective translation of the *Tao Te Ching* that is accessible to a modern Western audience. In spite of these difficulties, over forty translations exist in print in English alone, plus thirty or more online. However, a simple, side-by-side comparison of two or more translations will reveal the wide-ranging differences in interpretation adopted by individual translators, but this is hardly surprising in view of the enigmatic nature of the Tao itself and the ambiguous style of the *Tao Te Ching*.

John H. McDonald, the author of the translation presented here, consulted a number of different versions of the text in an attempt to find a consensus among them and produce a definitive translation of this ancient Chinese classic.

Most translations refer to the Sage or Master as being exclusively masculine in gender, but McDonald chose the feminine because 'a Master is aware of both, but chooses the least likely of the two', as the following verse shows:

*Know the masculine,*
*but keep to the feminine:*
*and become a watershed to the world.*
(CHAPTER 28)

# Lao Tzu

The little we know about Lao Tzu comes from the *Shi chi* (Records of the Historian) compiled towards the beginning of the 1st century BCE by the Han historian Ssu-ma Ch'ien (145–85 BCE).

The name 'Lao Tzu' is actually an honorific title meaning 'Old Master' – according to Ssu-ma Ch'ien, his given name was Li Er Tan. Born in the village of Chu Jen in the state of Ch'u, in later life he became an archivist at the court of the Chou Dynasty. Ssu-ma Ch'ien also recounts two events from Lao Tzu's life.

The first of these was a visit by Confucius, who asked Lao Tzu to tutor him in the traditional rites. Lao Tzu replied in words that express some of the central themes of the *Tao Te Ching*, saying, 'Those you talk about have turned to dust. All that remains is their words. When a nobleman lives in good times, he goes to court in a carriage. But when times are hard, he goes where the wind blows. Some people say that a wise merchant hides his wealth and thus appears to be poor. Likewise the sage: if he has great inner virtue, he appears outwardly to be a fool. Stop being so arrogant with all your questions, your self-importance and your overbearing obsessions. None of this is the real you. That is all I have to say to you.'

When Confucius rejoined his followers, he described his meeting with Lao Tzu thus: 'I know

that birds fly, fish swim and animals run. Creatures that run can be trapped; those that swim can be caught in nets; those that fly can be shot down. But what to do with a dragon, I do not know. It rides on the clouds and the wind. Today I met Lao Tzu, and he is like a dragon.'

The second event related by Ssu-ma Ch'ien is the final journey of Lao Tzu. Despairing at the moral decline of the kingdom and people's obsessive desire for possessions and status, Lao Tzu set off on a water buffalo to travel to the West. (According to some traditions he was withdrawing from the world to become a hermit, but the story takes on a slightly different meaning when we consider that in Chinese mythology 'the West' is the land of the afterlife.) When he reached the western gate of the kingdom in the mountain pass at Hang-ku, he was recognized as a sage by Kuan Yin, the Keeper of the Pass, who asked Lao Tzu to write down his knowledge of the Tao before retiring from the world. Lao Tzu duly obliged and, according to tradition, wrote the book in one night. The next day the sage presented the book to Kuan Yin, saying, 'This book is no different from other books in that it is a dead thing, but you can bring it to life if you put into practice what is written in it.' With that, Lao Tzu mounted his water buffalo and departed for the West, never to be seen again.

Whether or not a single individual known as Lao Tzu, the 'Old Master', was the author of the *Tao Te Ching* is now openly questioned by many scholars, as is his historical existence. Instead, it is suggested that the text is more in the nature of an anthology of sayings compiled over an extended period of time before taking its present form. What is beyond question, however, is the profound nature of the universal wisdom contained in this seminal work on the Tao.

## The *Tao Te Ching*

The *Tao Te Ching* is essentially about the Tao, but a number of related themes recur throughout the text.

The most significant of these are the Sage or Master, rulers and government, and non-action (*wu-wei*).

## The Tao

The Chinese word *Tao* is generally translated as 'the Way', the implication being that it refers to a spiritual way or path. It also has a much wider, more enigmatic meaning than this, as indicated by the opening lines of the *Tao Te Ching*:

*The tao that can be described
is not the eternal Tao.
The name that can be spoken
is not the eternal Name.* (1)

The *Tao Te Ching* goes on to tell us that the Tao is not only 'older than the concept of God' (4), it is both 'intangible and evasive' (21) and therefore beyond all concepts. It 'may be regarded as the Mother of the universe' (25) for 'it alone nourishes and completes all things' (41). The Tao 'has always existed' and is even 'beyond existing and not existing' (21), from which we can infer that the Tao denotes an ultimate 'way', the Way of Absolute Reality (i.e. reality purely and simply 'as it is', unadulterated by our concepts and opinions). Yet when the Tao is 'looked at, there is nothing for [people] to

see. When listened for, there is nothing for them to hear' (35). Moreover, 'the world cannot understand it' (62) since the Tao lies beyond the grasp of our normal understanding. Or, as the *Tao Te Ching* tells us elsewhere, 'our basic understandings are not from the Tao because they come from the depths of our misunderstanding' (38).

If we wish to increase our capacity for understanding and thereby draw closer to the Tao, we are advised to change our way of thinking because 'the more knowledge you seek, the less you will understand' (47). We are encouraged to follow the example of the Master who 'learns by unlearning, thus she is able to understand all things' (64).

## The Sage or Master

The Sage or Master is one who, having become 'unlearned' by emptying him- or herself of all concepts and opinions, is 'filled with the Tao [and] is like a newborn child' (55). Having 'attained unity with the Tao' (39), the Master no longer has a 'self' (13). That is to say, he or she has attained a state of consciousness which is very different from the state we normally experience because 'the Master has no mind of her own' (49). His or her consciousness is as one with the Tao which is itself 'without wants and desires' (34), and so the Master is no longer governed by the whims and desires of the ego: 'freed from desire, you can see the hidden mystery. By having desire, you can only see what is visibly real' (1). As the Master freely admits, 'I am different from ordinary people. I nurse from the Great Mother's [Tao's] breasts' (20).

*Once we have found the Mother,*
*we begin to know what Her children should be.*
*When we know we are the Mother's child,*
*we begin to guard the qualities of the Mother in us.*
    (52)

Because the Master is filled with the qualities or virtues of the Tao, we find the *Tao Te Ching* employing similar expressions for both – for example, the Tao is likened to 'the Uncarved Block' (28), while the Master, whose union with the Tao has brought about his or her completion, is 'whole as an uncarved block of wood' (15); the Tao 'never acts with force' (37), likewise the Master 'shuns the use of violence' (60); the Tao 'does not compete' (73) and 'the Tao of the Wise Person acts by not competing' (81).

# Rulers and government

The historian Ssu-ma Ch'ien relates Lao Tzu's departure for the West during a period of moral decline. As we have seen, however, Ssu-ma Ch'ien's traditional 6th-century BC dating for the writing of the *Tao Te Ching* differs from the scholastic view which places it much later, in the late 4th or early 3rd century BCE, during the aptly named Warring States Period (480-222 BCE) – a period when regional warlords sought to annex smaller states in the declining years of the Chou dynasty. Significantly, both datings point to the *Tao Te Ching* having been written during a time of moral and political decline – a fitting context for the guidance it offers to those who rule or govern.

According to the *Tao Te Ching*, 'the best leaders are those the people hardly know exist' (17); they 'become servants of their people' (68) for 'only he who is the lowest servant of the kingdom, is worthy of becoming its ruler' (78). Good government 'is unobtrusive' and thus enables the people to 'become whole' (58). It doesn't interfere with the people unnecessarily:

*Governing a large country*
*is like frying small fish.*
*Too much poking spoils the meat.* (60)

Wise rulers are those who 'follow the way of the Tao' (37), for 'if a ruler abides by its principles, then her people will willingly follow' (32).

# Non-action or *wu-wei*

The *Tao Te Ching* tells us that 'true sayings seem contradictory' (78), and there are possibly few sayings more contradictory than those relating to the principle of non-action or *wu-wei*. For example, we are advised to

*Act by not acting;*
*do by not doing.* (63)

And we are told that

*The Master... accomplishes much without*
*doing anything.* (47)

In mastering the ego or 'self' rather than allowing it to master him/her, the Master is freed from the need to act out of personal desire or self-interest and thus becomes an empty vehicle for the Tao. In this liberated state of 'being' rather than 'doing', the Master enjoys that ultimate freedom – the 'freedom of no-choice' – because he does nothing; it is the Tao which accomplishes things through him.

*For those who practise not-doing,*
*everything will fall into place.* (3)

The *Tao Te Ching* was written 2,500 years ago. In many respects the world is now a very different place, thanks to advances in science and technology, transport and communication, and the emergence of the global economy. Yet in others the world is much the same as it was in the Warring States Period, for we are still fighting wars, still thirsting

after power and status and still obsessed with the acquisition of wealth and possessions. In that respect, the timeless wisdom that lies at the heart of the *Tao Te Ching* is just as relevant today as it was 2,500 years ago.

*Embrace simplicity.*
*Put others first.*
*Desire little.* (19)

*Without opening your door,*
*you can know the whole world.*
*Without looking out of your window,*
*you can understand the way of the Tao.* (47)

**John Baldock**

# TAO
# TE
# CHING

道德經

## Lao Tzu

Translated by
John H. McDonald

**1**

道可道，非常道。名可名，非常名。無名天地之始；
有名萬物之母。故常無欲，以觀其妙；常有欲，
以觀其徼。此兩者，同出而異名，同謂之玄。
玄之又玄，眾妙之門。

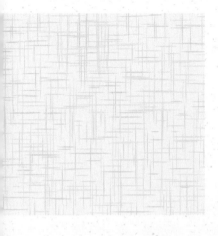

The tao that can be described
is not the eternal Tao.
The name that can be spoken
is not the eternal Name.

The nameless is the boundary of Heaven and Earth.
The named is the mother of creation.

Freed from desire, you can see the hidden mystery.
By having desire, you can only see what is visibly real.

Yet mystery and reality
emerge from the same source.
This source is called darkness.

Darkness born from darkness.
The beginning of all understanding.

2

天下皆知美之為美，斯惡已。皆知善之為善，
斯不善已。故有無相生，難易相成，長短相較，
高下相傾，音聲相和，前後相隨。是以聖人處無為
之事，行不言之教；萬物作焉而不辭，生而不有。
為而不恃，功成而弗居。夫唯弗居，是以不去。

When people see things as beautiful,
ugliness is created.
When people see things as good,
evil is created.

Being and non-being produce each other.
Difficult and easy complement each other.
Long and short define each other.
High and low oppose each other.
Fore and aft follow each other.

Therefore the Master
can act without doing anything
and teach without saying a word.
Things come her way and she does not
   stop them;
things leave and she lets them go.
She has without possessing,
and acts without any expectations.
When her work is done, she takes no credit.
That is why it will last forever.

不尚賢，使民不爭；不貴難
得之貨，使民不為盜；不見
可欲，使心不亂。是以聖人
之治，虛其心，實其腹，弱
其志，強其骨。常使民無知
無欲。使夫知者不敢為也。
為無為，則無不治。

If you over-esteem talented individuals,
people will become overly competitive.
If you overvalue possessions,
people will begin to steal.

Do not display your treasures
or people will become envious.

The Master leads by
emptying people's minds,
filling their bellies,
weakening their ambitions,
and making them become strong.
Preferring simplicity and freedom
    from desires,
avoiding the pitfalls of knowledge and
    wrong action.

For those who practise not-doing,
everything will fall into place.

**4**

道沖而用之或不盈。
淵兮似萬物之宗。挫其銳，
解其紛，和其光，同其塵。
湛兮似或存。吾不知誰之子，
象帝之先。

The Tao is like an empty container:
it can never be emptied and can never be filled.
Infinitely deep, it is the source of all things.
It dulls the sharp, unties the knotted,
shades the lighted, and unites all of creation
    with dust.

It is hidden but always present.
I don't know who gave birth to it.
It is older than the concept of God.

**5**

天地不仁，以萬物為芻狗；聖人不仁，以百姓為芻狗。天地之間，
其猶橐籥乎？虛而不屈，動而愈出。多言數窮，不如守中。

Heaven and Earth are impartial;
they treat all of creation as straw dogs.
The Master doesn't take sides;
she treats everyone like a straw dog.

The space between Heaven and Earth is like
    a bellows;
it is empty, yet has not lost its power.
The more it is used, the more it produces;
the more you talk of it, the less you comprehend.

It is better not to speak of things you do
    not understand.

**6**

谷神不死，是謂玄牝。玄牝之門，
是謂天地根。綿綿若存，用之不勤。

The spirit of emptiness is immortal.
It is called the Great Mother
because it gives birth to Heaven and Earth.

It is like a vapour,
barely seen but always present.
Use it effortlessly.

7

天長地久。天地所以能長且久者，以其不自生，
故能長生。是以聖人後其身而身先；外其身而身存。
非以其無私耶？故能成其私。

The Tao of Heaven is eternal,
and the earth is long enduring.
Why are they long enduring?
They do not live for themselves;
thus they are present for all beings.

The Master puts herself last;
And finds herself in the place of authority.
She detaches herself from all things;
Therefore she is united with all things.
She gives no thought to self.
She is perfectly fulfilled.

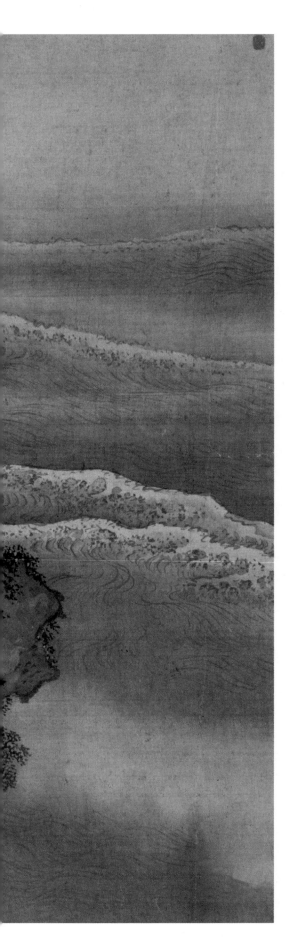

上善若水。水善利萬物而不爭，
處眾人之所惡，故幾於道。
居善地，心善淵，與善仁，
言善信，正善治，事善能，
動善時。夫唯不爭，故無尤。

The supreme good is like water,
which benefits all of creation
without trying to compete with it.
It gathers in unpopular places.
Thus it is like the Tao.

The location makes the dwelling good.
Depth of understanding makes the mind good.
A kind heart makes the giving good.
Integrity makes the government good.
Accomplishment makes your labours good.
Proper timing makes a decision good.

Only when there is no competition
will we all live in peace.

**9**

持而盈之，不如其已；揣而銳之，不可長保。
金玉滿堂，莫之能守；富貴而驕，自遺其咎。
功遂身退天之道。

It is easier to carry an empty cup
than one that is filled to the brim.

The sharper the knife
the easier it is to dull.
The more wealth you possess
the harder it is to protect.
Pride brings its own trouble.

When you have accomplished your goal
simply walk away.
This is the pathway to Heaven.

載營魄抱一，能無離乎？
專氣致柔，能嬰兒乎？
滌除玄覽，能無疵乎？
愛民治國，能無知乎？
天門開闔，能為雌乎？
明白四達，能無知乎？
生之、畜之，生而不有，
為而不恃，長而不宰，
是謂玄德。

**10**

Nurture the darkness of your soul
until you become whole.
Can you do this and not fail?
Can you focus your life-breath until you
    become
supple as a newborn child?
While you cleanse your inner vision
will you be found without fault?

Can you love people and lead them
without forcing your will on them?
When Heaven gives and takes away
can you be content with the outcome?
When you understand all things
can you step back from your own understanding?

Giving birth and nourishing,
making without possessing,
expecting nothing in return.
To grow, yet not to control:
This is the mysterious virtue.

三十輻，共一轂，
當其無，有車之用。
埏埴以為器，當其
無，有器之用。鑿戶
牖以為室，當其無，
有室之用。故有之以
為利，無之以為用。

Thirty spokes are joined together in a wheel,
but it is the centre hole
that allows the wheel to function.

We mould clay into a pot,
but it is the emptiness inside
that makes the vessel useful.

We fashion wood for a house,
but it is the emptiness inside
that makes it liveable.

We work with the substantial,
but the emptiness is what we use.

**12**

五色令人目盲；五音令人耳聾；五味令人口爽；
馳騁田獵，令人心發狂；難得之貨，令人行妨。
是以聖人為腹不為目，故去彼取此。

Five colours blind the eye.

Five notes deafen the ear.

Five flavours make the palate go stale.

Too much activity deranges the mind.

Too much wealth causes crime.

The Master acts on what she feels and
  not what she sees.

She shuns the latter, and prefers to
  seek the former.

寵辱若驚，
貴大患若身。
何謂寵辱若驚？
寵為下，得之若
驚，失之若驚，
是謂寵辱若驚。
何謂貴大患若身？
吾所以有大患者，
為吾有身，及吾
無身，吾有何患？
故貴以身為天下，
若可寄天下；
愛以身為天下，
若可託天下。

**13**

Success is as dangerous as failure,
and we are often our own worst enemy.

What does it mean that success is as dangerous as failure?
He who is superior is also someone's subordinate.
Receiving favour and losing it both cause alarm.
That is what is meant by 'success is as dangerous as failure'.
What does it mean that we are often our own worst enemy?
The reason I have an enemy is because I have a 'self'.
If I no longer had a 'self', I would no longer have an enemy.

Love the whole world as if it were your self;
then you will truly care for all things.

視之不見，名曰夷；聽之不聞，名曰希；搏之不得，名曰微。
此三者不可致詰，故混而為一。其上不皦，其下不昧。繩繩不可名，
復歸於無物。是謂無狀之狀，無物之象，是謂惚恍。迎之不見其首，
隨之不見其後。執古之道，以御今之有。能知古始，是謂道紀。

# 14

Look for it, and it can't be seen.
Listen for it, and it can't be heard.
Grasp for it, and it can't be caught.
These three cannot be further described,
so we treat them as The One.

Its highest is not bright.
Its depths are not dark.
Unending, unnameable, it returns to nothingness.
Formless forms, and imageless images,
subtle, beyond all understanding.

Approach it and you will not see a beginning;
follow it and there will be no end.
When we grasp the Tao of the ancient ones,
we can use it to direct our life today.
To know the ancient origin of Tao:
this is the beginning of wisdom.

**15**

古之善為士者，微妙玄通，
深不可識。夫唯不可識，
故強為之容。豫兮若冬涉川；
猶兮若畏四鄰；儼兮其若容；
渙兮若冰之將釋；敦兮其若樸；
曠兮其若谷；混兮其若濁；
孰能濁以靜之徐清？孰能安以久
動之徐生？保此道者，不欲盈。
夫唯不盈，故能蔽不新成。

The Sages of old were profound
and knew the ways of subtlety and discernment.
Their wisdom is beyond our comprehension.
Because their knowledge was so far superior
I can only give a poor description.

They were careful
as someone crossing a frozen stream in winter.
Alert as if surrounded on all sides by the enemy.
Courteous as a guest.
Fluid as melting ice.
Whole as an uncarved block of wood.
Receptive as a valley.
Turbid as muddied water.

Who can be still
until their mud settles
and the water is cleared by itself?
Can you remain tranquil until right action occurs by itself?

The Master doesn't seek fulfilment.
For only those who are not full are able to be used
which brings the feeling of completeness.

致虛極，守靜篤。萬物並作，吾以觀復。夫物芸芸，各復歸其根。歸根曰靜，是謂復命。復命曰常，知常曰明。不知常，妄作凶。知常容，容乃公，公乃王，王乃天，天乃道，道乃久，沒身不殆。

If you can empty your mind of all thoughts
your heart will embrace the tranquility of peace.
Watch the workings of all of creation,
but contemplate their return to the source.

All creatures in the universe
return to the point where they began.
Returning to the source is tranquility
because we submit to Heaven's mandate.

Returning to Heaven's mandate is called being constant.
Knowing the constant is called 'enlightenment'.
Not knowing the constant is the source of evil deeds
because we have no roots.
By knowing the constant we can accept things as they are.
By accepting things as they are, we become impartial.
By being impartial, we become one with Heaven.
By being one with Heaven, we become one with Tao.
Being one with Tao, we are no longer concerned about
losing our life because we know the Tao is constant
and we are one with Tao.

太上，下知有之；其次，親而譽之；其次，
畏之；其次，侮之。信不足，焉有不信焉。
悠兮，其貴言。功成事遂，百姓皆謂我自然。

The best leaders are those the people hardly know exist.
The next best is a leader who is loved and praised.
Next comes the one who is feared.
The worst one is the leader who is despised.

If you don't trust the people,
they will become untrustworthy.

The best leaders value their words, and use them sparingly.
When the Master has accomplished her task,
the people say, 'Amazing:
we did it, all by ourselves!'

**18** 大道廢，有仁義；智慧出，有大偽；六親不和，有孝慈；國家昏亂，有忠臣。

When the great Tao is abandoned,
charity and righteousness appear.
When intellectualism arises,
hypocrisy is close behind.

When there is strife in the family unit,
people talk about 'brotherly love'.

When the country falls into chaos,
politicians talk about 'patriotism'.

**19**

絕聖棄智，民利百倍；絕仁棄義，民復孝慈；
絕巧棄利，盜賊無有。此三者以為文不足。
故令有所屬：見素抱樸，少私寡欲。

Forget about knowledge and wisdom,
and people will be a hundred times better off.
Throw away charity and righteousness,
and people will return to brotherly love.
Throw away profit and greed,
and there won't be any thieves.

These three are superficial and aren't enough
to keep us at the centre of the circle, so we must also:

Embrace simplicity.
Put others first.
Desire little.

**20**

絕學無憂，唯之
與阿，相去幾何？
善之與惡，相去
若何？人之所畏，
不可不畏。荒兮
其未央哉！眾人熙
熙，如享太牢，
如春登臺。我獨怕
兮其未兆；如嬰兒
之未孩；儽儽兮若
無所歸。眾人皆有
餘，而我獨若遺。
我愚人之心也哉！
沌沌兮，俗人昭
昭，我獨若昏。

Renounce knowledge and your problems will end.
What is the difference between yes and no?
What is the difference between good and evil?
Must you fear what others fear?
Nonsense, look how far you have missed the mark!

Other people are joyous,
as though they were at a spring festival.
I alone am unconcerned and expressionless,
like an infant before it has learned to smile.
Other people have more than they need;
I alone seem to possess nothing.
I am lost and drift about with no place to go.
I am like a fool, my mind is in chaos.

俗人察察，我獨悶悶。
澹兮其若海，飂兮若無止，
眾人皆有以，而我獨頑似鄙。
我獨異於人，而貴食母。

Ordinary people are bright;
I alone am dark.
Ordinary people are clever;
I alone am dull.
Ordinary people seem discriminating;
I alone am muddled and confused.
I drift on the waves on the ocean,
blown at the mercy of the wind.
Other people have their goals,
I alone am dull and uncouth.

I am different from ordinary people.
I nurse from the Great Mother's breasts.

**21**

孔德之容，唯道是從。道之為物，唯恍唯惚。
忽兮恍兮，其中有象；恍兮忽兮，其中有物。
窈兮冥兮，其中有精；其精甚真，其中有信。
自古及今，其名不去，以閱眾甫。
吾何以知眾甫之狀哉？以此。

The greatest virtue you can have
comes from following only the Tao;
which takes a form that is intangible and evasive.

Even though the Tao is intangible and evasive,
we are able to know it exists.
Intangible and evasive, yet it has a manifestation.
Secluded and dark, yet there is a vitality within it.
Its vitality is very genuine.
Within it we can find order.

Since the beginning of time, the Tao has always existed.
It is beyond existing and not existing.
How do I know where creation comes from?
I look inside myself and see it.

曲則全，枉則直，窪則盈，
弊則新，少則得，多則惑。
是以聖人抱一為天下式。
不自見，故明；不自是，
故彰；不自伐，故有功；
不自矜，故長。夫唯不爭，
故天下莫能與之爭。
古之所謂曲則全者，
豈虛言哉！誠全而歸之。

If you want to become whole,
first let yourself become broken.
If you want to become straight,
first let yourself become twisted.
If you want to become full,
first let yourself become empty.
If you want to become new,
first let yourself become old.
Those whose desires are few get them,
those whose desires are great go astray.

For this reason the Master embraces the Tao,
as an example for the world to follow.
Because she isn't self-centred,
people can see the light in her.
Because she does not boast of herself,
she becomes a shining example.
Because she does not glorify herself,
she becomes a person of merit.
Because she wants nothing from the world,
the world cannot overcome her.
When the ancient Masters said,
'If you want to become whole,
then first let yourself be broken,'
they weren't using empty words.
All who do this will be made complete.

**23**

希言自然，故飄風不終朝，驟雨不終日。孰為此者？
天地。天地尚不能久，而況於人乎？故從事於道者，
道者，同於道；德者，同於德；失者，同於失。
同於道者，道亦樂得之；同於德者，德亦樂得之；
同於失者，失亦樂得之。信不足，焉有不信焉。

Nature uses few words:
when the gale blows, it will not last long;
when it rains hard, it lasts but a little while;
What causes these to happen? Heaven and Earth.

Why do we humans go on endlessly about little
when nature does much in a little time?
If you open yourself to the Tao,
you and Tao become one.
If you open yourself to Virtue,
then you can become virtuous.
If you open yourself to loss,
then you will become lost.

If you open yourself to the Tao,
the Tao will eagerly welcome you.
If you open yourself to virtue,
virtue will become a part of you.
If you open yourself to loss,
the lost are glad to see you.

When you do not trust people,
people will become untrustworthy.

企者不立；跨者不行；自見者不明；自是者不彰；
自伐者無功；自矜者不長。其在道也，
曰：餘食贅行。物或惡之，故有道者不處。

**24**

Those who stand on tiptoes
do not stand firmly.
Those who rush ahead
don't get very far.
Those who try to outshine others
dim their own light.
Those who call themselves righteous
can't know how wrong they are.
Those who boast of their accomplishments
diminish the things they have done.

Compared to the Tao, these actions are unworthy.
If we are to follow the Tao, we must not do these things.

## 25

有物混成，先天地生。寂兮寥兮，
獨立不改，周行而不殆，可以為天下
母。吾不知其名，字之曰道，強為之
名曰大。大曰逝，逝曰遠，遠曰反。
故道大，天大，地大，王亦大。域中
有四大，而王居其一焉。人法地，
地法天，天法道，道法自然。

Before the universe was born
there was something in the chaos of the heavens.
It stands alone and empty,
solitary and unchanging.
It is ever present and secure.
It may be regarded as the Mother of the universe.
Because I do not know its name,
I call it the Tao.
If forced to give it a name,
I would call it 'Great'.

Because it is Great means it is everywhere.
Being everywhere means it is eternal.
Being eternal means everything returns to it.

Tao is great.
Heaven is great.
Earth is great.
Humanity is great.
Within the universe, these are the four great things.

Humanity follows the earth.
Earth follows Heaven.
Heaven follows the Tao.
The Tao follows only itself.

重為輕根，靜為躁君。是以聖人終日行不離輜重。雖有榮觀，
燕處超然。奈何萬乘之主，而以身輕天下？輕則失本，躁則失君。

**26**

Heaviness is the basis of lightness.
Stillness is the standard of activity.

Thus the Master travels all day
without ever leaving her wagon.
Even though she has much to see,
she is at peace in her indifference.

Why should the lord of a thousand chariots
be amused at the foolishness of the world?
If you abandon yourself to foolishness,
you lose touch with your beginnings.
If you let yourself become distracted,
you will lose the basis of your power.

**27**

善行無轍迹，善言無瑕讁；
善數不用籌策；
善閉無關楗而不可開，
善結無繩約而不可解。
是以聖人常善救人，
故無棄人；常善救物，
故無棄物。是謂襲明。
故善人者，不善人之師；
不善人者，善人之資。
不貴其師，不愛其資，
雖智大迷，是謂要妙。

A good traveller leaves no tracks,
and a skilful speaker is well rehearsed.
A good bookkeeper has an excellent memory,
and a well-made door is easy to open and needs no locks.
A good knot needs no rope and it can not come undone.

Thus the Master is willing to help everyone,
and doesn't know the meaning of rejection.
She is there to help all of creation,
and doesn't abandon even the smallest creature.
This is called embracing the light.

What is a good person but a bad person's teacher?
What is a bad person but raw material for his teacher?
If you fail to honour your teacher or fail to enjoy your student,
you will become deluded no matter how smart you are.
It is the secret of prime importance.

知其雄，守其雌，
為天下谿。為天下谿，
常德不離，復歸於嬰兒。
知其白，守其黑，
為天下式。為天下式，
常德不忒，復歸於無極。

Know the masculine,
but keep to the feminine:
and become a watershed to the world.
If you embrace the world,
the Tao will never leave you
and you become as a little child.

Know the white,
yet keep to the black:
be a model for the world.
If you are a model for the world,
the Tao inside you will strengthen
and you will return whole to your eternal beginning.

知其榮，守其辱，
為天下谷。為天下谷，
常德乃足，復歸於樸。
樸散則為器，聖人用之，
則為官長，故大制不割。

Know the honourable,
but do not shun the disgraced:
embrace the world as it is.
If you embrace the world with compassion,
then your virtue will return you to the
Uncarved Block.

The block of wood is carved into utensils
by carving a void into the wood.
The Master uses the utensils, yet prefers to keep to the block
because of its limitless possibilities.
Great works do not involve discarding substance.

29

將欲取天下而為之，
吾見其不得已。天下
神器，不可為也，為
者敗之，執者失之。
故物或行或隨；或歔
或吹；或強或羸；或
挫或隳。是以聖人去
甚，去奢，去泰。

Do you want to rule the world and control it?
I don't think it can ever be done.

The world is a sacred vessel
and it can not be controlled.
You will only make it worse if you try.
It may slip through your fingers and disappear.

Some are meant to lead,
and others are meant to follow;
Some must always strain,
and others have an easy time;
Some are naturally big and strong,
and others will always be small;
Some will be protected and nurtured,
and others will meet with destruction.

The Master accepts things as they are,
and out of compassion avoids extravagance,
excess and the extremes.

以道佐人主者，
不以兵強天下。
其事好還。師之
所處，荊棘生
焉。大軍之後，
必有凶年。善有
果而已，不敢以
取強。果而勿
矜，果而勿伐，
果而勿驕。果而
不得已，果而勿
強。物壯則老，
是謂不道，
不道早已。

Those who lead people by following the Tao
don't use weapons to enforce their will.
Using force always leads to unseen troubles.

In the places where armies march,
thorns and briars bloom and grow.
After armies take to war,
bad years must always follow.
The skilful commander
strikes a decisive blow then stops.
When victory is won over the enemy through war
it is not a thing of great pride.
When the battle is over,
arrogance is the new enemy.
War can result when no other alternative is given,
so the one who overcomes an enemy should not dominate them.
The strong are always weakened with time.

This is not the way of the Tao.
That which is not of the Tao will soon end.

夫佳兵者，不祥之器，物或惡之，
故有道者不處。君子居則貴左，用兵則
貴右。兵者不祥之器，非君子之器，
不得已而用之，恬淡為上。勝而不美，
而美之者，是樂殺人。夫樂殺人者，
則不可以得志於天下矣。

## 31

Weapons are the bearers of bad news;
all people should detest them.

The wise man values the left side,
and in a time of war he values the right.
Weapons are meant for destruction,
and thus are avoided by the wise.
Only as a last resort
will a wise person use a deadly weapon.
If peace is her true objective
how can she rejoice in the victory of war?
Those who rejoice in victory
delight in the slaughter of humanity.
Those who resort to violence
will never bring peace to the world.

吉事尚左，凶事尚右。
偏將軍居左，上將軍居右，
言以喪禮處之。殺人之衆，
以哀悲泣之，戰勝以喪禮處之。

The left side is a place of honour on happy occasions.
The right side is reserved for mourning at a funeral.
When the lieutenants take the left side to prepare for war,
the general should be on the right side,
because he knows the outcome will be death.
The death of many should be greeted with great sorrow,
and the victory celebration should honour those who have died.

**32**

道常無名。樸雖小，天下莫能臣也。侯王若能守之，
萬物將自賓。天地相合，以降甘露，民莫之令而自均。
始制有名，名亦既有，夫亦將知止，知止所以不殆。
譬道之在天下，猶川谷之與江海。

The Tao is nameless and unchanging.
Although it appears insignificant,
nothing in the world can contain it.

If a ruler abides by its principles,
then her people will willingly follow.
Heaven would then reign on earth,
like sweet rain falling on paradise.
People would have no need for laws,
because the law would be written on their hearts.

Naming is a necessity for order,
but naming can not order all things.
Naming often makes things impersonal,
so we should know when naming should end.
Knowing when to stop naming,
you can avoid the pitfall it brings.

All things end in the Tao
just as the small streams and the largest rivers
flow through valleys to the sea.

知人者智，自知者明。勝人者有力，
自勝者強。知足者富。強行者有志。
不失其所者久。死而不亡者壽。

Those who know others are intelligent;
those who know themselves are truly wise.
Those who master others are strong;
those who master themselves have true power.

Those who know they have enough are truly wealthy.

Those who persist will reach their goal.

Those who keep their course have a strong will.
Those who embrace death will not perish,
but have life everlasting.

大道汜兮，其可左右。萬物恃之而生而不辭，
功成不名有。衣養萬物而不為主，常無欲，
可名於小；萬物歸焉，而不為主，可名為大。
以其終不自為大，故能成其大。

The great Tao flows unobstructed in every direction.

All things rely on it to conceive and be born,

and it does not deny even the smallest of creation.

When it has accomplished great wonders,

it does not claim them for itself.

It nourishes infinite worlds,

yet it doesn't seek to master the smallest creature.

Since it is without wants and desires,

it can be considered humble.

All of creation seeks it for refuge

yet it does not seek to master or control.

Because it does not seek greatness,

it is able to accomplish truly great things.

執大象，天下往。往而不害，安平大。樂與餌，
過客止。道之出口，淡乎其無味，視之不足見，
聽之不足聞，用之不足既。

**35**

She who follows the way of the Tao
will draw the world to her steps.
She can go without fear of being injured,
because she has found peace and tranquility in her heart.

Where there is music and good food,
people will stop to enjoy it.
But words spoken of the Tao
seem to them boring and stale.
When looked at, there is nothing for them to see.
When listened for, there is nothing for them to hear.
Yet if they put it to use, it would never be exhausted.

36

將欲歙之，必固張之；
將欲弱之，必固強之；
將欲廢之，必固興之；
將欲奪之，必固與之。
是謂微明。柔弱勝剛
強。魚不可脫於淵，
國之利器不可以示人。

If you want something to return to the source,
you must first allow it to spread out.
If you want something to weaken,
you must first allow it to become strong.
If you want something to be removed,
you must first allow it to flourish.
If you want to possess something,
you must first give it away.

This is called the subtle understanding
of how things are meant to be.

The soft and pliable overcomes the hard and inflexible.

Just as fish remain hidden in deep waters,
it is best to keep weapons out of sight.

**37**

道常無為而無不為。侯王若能守之，
萬物將自化。化而欲作，
吾將鎮之以無名之樸。無名之樸，
夫亦將無欲。不欲以静，天下將自定。

The Tao never acts with force,
yet there is nothing that it cannot do.

If rulers could follow the way of the Tao,
then all of creation would willingly follow their example.
If selfish desires were to arise after their transformation,
I would erase them with the power of the Uncarved Block.

By the power of the Uncarved Block,
future generations would lose their selfish desires.
By losing their selfish desires,
the world would naturally settle into peace.

38

上德不德，是以有德；下德不失德，是以無德。
上德無為而無以為；下德為之而有以為。
上仁為之而無以為；上義為之而有以為。
上禮為之而莫之應，則攘臂而扔之。

The highest good is not to seek to do good,
but to allow yourself to become it.
The ordinary person seeks to do good things,
and finds that they can not do them continually.

The Master does not force virtue on others,
thus she is able to accomplish her task.
The ordinary person who uses force,
will find that they accomplish nothing.

The kind person acts from the heart,
and accomplishes a multitude of things.
The righteous person acts out of pity,
yet leaves many things undone.
The moral person will act out of duty,
and when no one responds
will roll up his sleeves and use force.

故失道而後德，失德而後仁，
失仁而後義，失義而後禮。
夫禮者，忠信之薄，而亂之首。
前識者，道之華，而愚之始。
是以大丈夫處其厚，不居其薄；
處其實，不居其華。故去彼取此。

When the Tao is forgotten, there is righteousness.
When righteousness is forgotten, there is morality.
When morality is forgotten, there is the law.
The law is the husk of faith,
and trust is the beginning of chaos.

Our basic understandings are not from the Tao
because they come from the depths of our
    misunderstanding.
The master abides in the fruit and not in the husk.
She dwells in the Tao,
and not with the things that hide it.
This is how she increases in wisdom.

昔之得一者：天得一以清；
地得一以寧；神得一以靈；
谷得一以盈；萬物得一以生；
侯王得一以為天下貞。

**39**

The masters of old attained unity with the Tao.
Heaven attained unity and became pure.
The earth attained unity and found peace.
The spirits attained unity so they could minister.
The valleys attained unity that they might be full.
Humanity attained unity that they might flourish.
Their leaders attained unity that they might set
    the example.
This is the power of unity.

其致之，天無以清，將恐裂；地無以
寧，將恐發；神無以靈，將恐歇；
谷無以盈，將恐竭；萬物無以生，
將恐滅；侯王無以貴高將恐蹶。
故貴以賤為本，高以下為基。
是以侯王自稱孤、寡、不穀。
此非以賤為本耶？非乎？故致數譽
無譽。不欲琭琭如玉，珞珞如石。

Without unity, the sky becomes filthy.
Without unity, the earth becomes unstable.
Without unity, the spirits become unresponsive
    and disappear.
Without unity, the valleys become dry as a desert.
Without unity, humankind can't reproduce and
    becomes extinct.
Without unity, our leaders become corrupt and fall.

The great view the small as their source,
and the high take the low as their foundation.
Their greatest asset becomes their humility.
They speak of themselves as orphans and widows,
thus they truly seek humility.
Do not shine like the precious gem,
but be as dull as a common stone.

## 40

反者道之動；
弱者道之用。
天下萬物生於有，
有生於無。

All movement returns to the Tao.
Weakness is how the Tao works.

All of creation is born from substance.
Substance is born of nothing-ness.

上士聞道，勤而行之；
中士聞道，若存若亡；
下士聞道，大笑之。
不笑不足以為道。
故建言有之：明道若昧；
進道若退；夷道若纇；
上德若谷；太白若辱；
廣德若不足；建德若偷；
質真若渝；大方無隅；
大器晚成；大音希聲；
大象無形；道隱無名。
夫唯道，善貸且成。

When a superior person hears of the Tao,
She diligently puts it into practice.
When an average person hears of the Tao,
he believes half of it, and doubts the other half.
When a foolish person hears of the Tao,
he laughs out loud at the very idea.
If he didn't laugh,
it wouldn't be the Tao.

Thus it is said:
The brightness of the Tao seems like darkness,
the advancement of the Tao seems like retreat,
the level path seems rough,
the superior path seems empty,
the pure seems to be tarnished,
and true virtue doesn't seem to be enough.
The virtue of caution seems like cowardice,
the pure seems to be polluted,
the true square seems to have no corners,
the best vessels take the most time to finish,
the greatest sounds cannot be heard,
and the greatest image has no form.

The Tao hides in the unnamed,
Yet it alone nourishes and completes all things.

**42**

道生一，一生二，二生三，三生萬物。
萬物負陰而抱陽，沖氣以為和。人之所惡，
唯孤、寡、不穀，而王公以為稱。
故物或損之而益，或益之而損。
人之所教，我亦教之。
強梁者不得其死，吾將以為教父。

The Tao gave birth to One.
The One gave birth to Two.
The Two gave birth to Three.
The Three gave birth to all of creation.

All things carry Yin
yet embrace Yang.
They blend their life breaths
in order to produce harmony.

People despise being orphaned, widowed and poor.
But the noble ones take these as their titles.
In losing, much is gained,
and, in gaining, much is lost.

What others teach I too will teach:
'The strong and violent will not die a natural death.'

**43**

天下之至柔，馳騁天下
之至堅。無有入無間，
吾是以知無為之有益。
不言之教，無為之益，
天下希及之。

That which offers no resistance
overcomes the hardest substances.
That which offers no resistance
can enter where there is no space.

Few in the world can comprehend
the teaching without words,
or understand the value of non-action.

44

Which is more important, your honour or your life?
Which is more valuable, your possessions or your person?
Which is more destructive, success or failure?

Great love extracts a great cost
and true wealth requires greater loss.

名與身孰親？
身與貨孰多？
得與亡孰病？
是故甚愛必大費；
多藏必厚亡。
知足不辱，
知止不殆，
可以長久。

Knowing when you have enough avoids dishonour,
and knowing when to stop will keep you from danger
and bring you a long, happy life.

大成若缺，其用不弊。
大盈若沖，其用不窮。
大直若屈，大巧若拙，大辯若訥。
躁勝寒靜勝熱。清靜為天下正。

**45**

The greatest accomplishments seem imperfect,
yet their usefulness is not diminished.
The greatest fullness seems empty,
yet it will be inexhaustible.

The greatest straightness seems crooked.
The most valued skill seems like clumsiness.
The greatest speech seems full of stammers.

Movement overcomes the cold,
and stillness overcomes the heat.
That which is pure and still is the universal ideal.

天下有道，卻走馬以糞。
天下無道，戎馬生於郊。
禍莫大於不知足；咎莫大於欲得。
故知足之足，常足矣。

When the world follows the Tao,
horses run free to fertilize the fields.
When the world does not follow the Tao,
war horses are bred outside the cities.

There is no greater transgression
than condoning people's selfish desires,
no greater disaster than being discontent,
and no greater retribution than for greed.

Whoever knows contentment will be at peace forever.

不出戶知天下；
不闚牖見天道。
其出彌遠，
其知彌少。
是以聖人不行而知，
不見而名，
不為而成。

Without opening your door,
you can know the whole world.
Without looking out of your window,
you can understand the way of the Tao.

The more knowledge you seek,
the less you will understand.

The Master understands without leaving,
sees clearly without looking,
accomplishes much without doing anything.

**48**

One who seeks knowledge learns something new every day.
One who seeks the Tao unlearns something new every day.
Less and less remains until you arrive at non-action.
When you arrive at non-action,
nothing will be left undone.

為學日益，
為道日損。
損之又損，
以至於無為。
無為而無不為。
取天下常以無事，
及其有事，
不足以取天下。

Mastery of the world is achieved
by letting things take their natural course.
You can not master the world by changing the natural way.

**49**

聖人無常心，以百姓心
為心。善者，吾善之；
不善者，吾亦善之；
德善。信者，吾信之；
不信者，吾亦信之；
德信。聖人在天下，
歙歙為天下渾其心，
百姓皆注其耳目，
聖人皆孩之。

The Master has no mind of her own.
She understands the mind of the people.

Those who are good she treats as good.
Those who aren't good she also treats as good.
This is how she attains true goodness.

She trusts people who are trustworthy.
She also trusts people who aren't trustworthy.
This is how she gains true trust.

The Master's mind is shut off from the world.
Only for the sake of the people does she
    muddle her mind.
They look to her in anticipation. Yet she treats
    them all as her children.

**50**

出生入死。生之徒，十有三；死之徒，十有三；
人之生，動之死地，十有三。夫何故？以其生，
生之厚。蓋聞善攝生者，陸行不遇兕虎，
入軍不被甲兵；兕無所投其角，虎無所措其爪，
兵無所容其刃。夫何故？以其無死地。

Those who leave the womb at birth
and those who enter their source at death,
of these; three out of ten celebrate life,
three out of ten celebrate death,
and three out of ten simply go from life to death.
What is the reason for this?
Because they are afraid of dying,
therefore they cannot live.

I have heard that those who celebrate life
walk safely among the wild animals.
When they go into battle, they remain unharmed.
The animals find no place to attack them
and the weapons are unable to harm them.
Why? Because they can find no place for death in them.

道生之，德畜之，物形之，勢成之。是以萬物莫不尊道而貴德。
道之尊，德之貴，夫莫之命常自然。故道生之，德畜之；長之育之；
亭之毒之；養之覆之。生而不有，為而不恃，長而不宰，是謂玄德。

**51**

The Tao gives birth to all of creation.
The virtue of Tao in nature nurtures them,
and their family gives them their form.
Their environment then shapes them into completion.
That is why every creature honours the Tao and its virtue.

No one tells them to honour the Tao and its virtue,
it happens all by itself.
So the Tao gives them birth,
and its virtue cultivates them,
cares for them,
nurtures them,
gives them a place of refuge and peace,
helps them to grow and shelters them.

It gives them life without wanting to possess them,
and cares for them expecting nothing in return.
It is their master, but it does not seek to dominate them.
This is called the dark and mysterious virtue.

**52**

天下有始，以為天下母。既得其母，以知其子，
既知其子，復守其母，沒身不殆。塞其兌，閉其門，
終身不勤。開其兌，濟其事，終身不救。見小曰明，
守柔曰強。用其光，復歸其明，無遺身殃；是為習常。

The world had a beginning
which we call the Great Mother.
Once we have found the Mother,
we begin to know what Her children should be.

When we know we are the Mother's child,
we begin to guard the qualities of the Mother in us.
She will protect us from all danger
even if we lose our life.

Keep your mouth closed
and embrace a simple life,
and you will live care-free until the end of your days.
If you try to talk your way into a better life
there will be no end to your trouble.

To understand the small is called clarity.
Knowing how to yield is called strength.
To use your inner light for understanding
regardless of the danger
is called depending on the Constant.

使我介然有知，行於大道，
唯施是畏。大道甚夷，
而民好徑。朝甚除，
田甚蕪，倉甚虛；服文綵，
帶利劍，厭飲食，財貨有餘；
是謂盜夸。非道也哉！

**53**

If I understood only one thing,
I would want to use it to follow the Tao.
My only fear would be one of pride.
The Tao goes in the level places,
but people prefer to take the short cuts.

If too much time is spent cleaning the house
the land will become neglected and full of weeds,
and the granaries will soon become empty
because there is no one out working the fields.
To wear fancy clothes and ornaments,
to have your fill of food and drink
and to waste all of your money buying possessions
is called the crime of excess.
Oh, how these things go against the way of the Tao!

善建不拔，善抱者
不脫，子孫以祭祀
不輟。修之於身，
其德乃真；修之
於家，其德乃餘；
修之於鄉，其德乃
長；修之於國，
其德乃豐；修之於
天下，其德乃普。
故以身觀身，以家
觀家，以鄉觀鄉，
以國觀國，以天下
觀天下。吾何以知
天下然哉？以此。

That which is well built
will never be torn down.
That which is well latched
can not slip away.
Those who do things well
will be honoured from generation to generation.

If this idea is cultivated in the individual,
then his virtue will become genuine.
If this idea is cultivated in your family,
then virtue in your family will be great.
If this idea is cultivated in your community,
then virtue will go a long way.
If this idea is cultivated in your country,
then virtue will be in many places.
If this idea is cultivated in the world,
then virtue will be with everyone.

Then observe the person for what the person does,
and observe the family for what it does,
and observe the community for what it does,
and observe the country for what it does,
and observe the world for what it does.
How do I know this saying is true?
I observe these things and see.

**55**

含德之厚，比於赤子。蜂蠆虺蛇不螫，
猛獸不據，攫鳥不搏。骨弱筋柔而握固。
未知牝牡之合而全作，精之至也。
終日號而不嗄，和之至也。知和曰常，
知常曰明，益生曰祥。心使氣曰強。
物壯則老，謂之不道，不道早已。

One who is filled with the Tao
is like a newborn child.
The infant is protected from
the stinging insects, wild beasts, and birds of prey.
Its bones are soft, its muscles are weak,
but its grip is firm and strong.
It doesn't know about the union
of male and female,
yet his penis can stand erect
because of the power of life within him.
It can cry all day and never become hoarse.
This is perfect harmony.

To understand harmony is to understand the Constant.
To know the Constant is to be called 'enlightened'.
To unnaturally try to extend life is not appropriate.
To try and alter the life-breath is unnatural.
The master understands that when something reaches its prime
it will soon begin to decline.
Changing the natural is against the way of the Tao.
Those who do it will come to an early end.

**56**

知者不言，
言者不知。
塞其兌，閉其門，
挫其銳，解其分，
和其光，同其塵，
是謂玄同。
故不可得而親，
不可得而疎；
不可得而利，
不可得而害；
不可得而貴，
不可得而賤。
故為天下貴。

Those who know do not talk.
Those who talk do not know.

Stop talking,
meditate in silence,
blunt your sharpness,
release your worries,
harmonize your inner light,
and become one with the dust.
Doing this is called the dark and mysterious identity.

Those who have achieved the mysterious identity
can not be approached, and they can not be alienated.
They can not be benefited nor harmed.
They can not be made noble nor to suffer disgrace.
This makes them the most noble of all under the heavens.

57

以正治國，以奇用兵，
以無事取天下。
吾何以知其然哉？
以此：天下多忌諱，
而民彌貧；民多利器，
國家滋昏；人多伎巧，
奇物滋起；法令滋彰，
盜賊多有。故聖人云：
我無為，而民自化；
我好靜，而民自正；
我無事，而民自富；
我無欲，而民自樸。

Govern your country with integrity,
Weapons of war can be used with great cunning,
but loyalty is only won by not-doing.
How do I know the way things are?
By these:

The more prohibitions you make,
the poorer people will be.
The more weapons you possess,
the greater the chaos in your country.
The more knowledge that is acquired,
the stranger the world will become.
The more laws that you make,
the greater the number of criminals.

Therefore the Master says:
I do nothing,
and people become good by themselves.
I seek peace,
and people take care of their own problems.
I do not meddle in their personal lives,
and the people become prosperous.
I let go of all my desires,
and the people return to the Uncarved Block.

其政悶悶，其民淳淳；其政察察，
其民缺缺。禍兮福之所倚，福兮禍之所伏。
孰知其極？其無正。正復為奇，善復為妖。
人之迷，其日固久。是以聖人方而不割，
廉而不劌，直而不肆，光而不燿。

**58**

If a government is unobtrusive,
the people become whole.
If a government is repressive,
the people become treacherous.

Good fortune has its roots in disaster,
and disaster lurks with good fortune.
Who knows why these things happen,
or when this cycle will end?
Good things seem to change into bad,
and bad things often turn out for good.
These things have always been hard to comprehend.

Thus the Master makes things change
without interfering.
She is probing yet causes no harm.
Straightforward, yet does not impose her will.
Radiant, and easy on the eye.

治人事天莫若嗇。夫唯嗇，是謂早服；早服謂之重積德；
重積德則無不克；無不克則莫知其極；莫知其極，可以有國；
有國之母，可以長久；是謂深根固柢，長生久視之道。

**59**

There is nothing better than moderation
for teaching people or serving Heaven.
Those who use moderation
are already on the path to the Tao.

Those who follow the Tao early
will have an abundance of virtue.
When there is an abundance of virtue,
there is nothing that cannot be done.
Where there is limitless ability,
then the kingdom is within your grasp.
When you know the Mother of the kingdom,
then you will be long enduring.

This is spoken of as the deep root and the firm trunk,
the Way to a long life and great spiritual vision.

治大國若烹小鮮。以道蒞天下，其鬼不神；
非其鬼不神，其神不傷人；非其神不傷人，
聖人亦不傷人。夫兩不相傷，故德交歸焉。

Governing a large country
is like frying small fish.
Too much poking spoils the meat.

When the Tao is used to govern the world
then evil will lose its power to harm the people.
Not that evil will no longer exist,
but only because it has lost its power.
Just as evil can lose its ability to harm,
the Master shuns the use of violence.

If you give evil nothing to oppose,
then virtue will return by itself.

**61**

大國者下流，天下之交，天下之牝。牝常以靜勝牡，
以靜為下。故大國以下小國，則取小國；
小國以下大國，則取大國。故或下以取，或下而取。
大國不過欲兼畜人，小國不過欲入事人。
夫兩者各得其所欲，大者宜為下。

A large country should take the low place like a great watershed,
which from its low position assumes the female role.
The female overcomes the male by the power of her position.
Her tranquility gives rise to her humility.

If a large country takes the low position,
it will be able to influence smaller countries.
If smaller countries take the lower position,
then they can allow themselves to be influenced.
So both seek to take the lower position
in order to influence the other, or be influenced.

Large countries should desire to protect and help the people,
and small countries should desire to serve others.
Both large and small countries benefit greatly from humility.

**62**

The Tao is the tabernacle of creation,
it is a treasure for those who are good,
and a place of refuge for those who are not.

How can those who are not good be abandoned?
Words that are beautiful are worth much,
but good behaviour can only be learned by example.

道者萬物之奧。
善人之寶，不善人
之所保。美言可以市，
尊行可以加人。
人之不善，何棄之有？
故立天子，置三公，
雖有拱璧以先駟馬，
不如坐進此道。
古之所以貴此道者何？
不曰：以求得，
有罪以免耶？
故為天下貴。

When a new leader takes office,
don't give him gifts and offerings.
These things are not as valuable
as teaching him about the Tao.

Why was the Tao esteemed by the ancient Masters?
Is it not said: 'With it we find without looking.
With it we find forgiveness for our transgressions'?
That is why the world cannot understand it.

**63**

為無為，事無事，味無味。大小多少，報怨以德。
圖難於其易，為大於其細；天下難事，必作於易，
天下大事，必作於細。是以聖人終不為大，
故能成其大。夫輕諾必寡信，多易必多難。
是以聖人猶難之，故終無難矣。

Act by not acting;
do by not doing.
Enjoy the plain and simple.
Find that greatness in the small.
Take care of difficult problems
while they are still easy;
Do easy things before they become too hard.

Difficult problems are best solved while they are easy.
Great projects are best started while they are small.
The Master never takes on more than she can handle,
which means that she leaves nothing undone.

When an affirmation is given too lightly,
keep your eyes open for trouble ahead.
When something seems too easy,
difficulty is hiding in the details.
The Master expects great difficulty,
so the task is always easier than planned.

**64**

其安易持，其未兆易謀。其脆易泮，其微易散。
為之於未有，治之於未亂。合抱之木，生於毫末；
九層之臺，起於累土；千里之行，始於足下。
為者敗之，執者失之。

Things are easier to control while they are quiet.
Things are easier to plan far in advance.
Things break easier while they are still brittle.
Things are easier hid while they are still small.

Prevent problems before they arise.

Take action before things get out of hand.

The tallest tree

begins as a tiny sprout.

The tallest building

starts with one shovel of dirt.

A journey of a thousand miles

starts with a single footstep.

If you rush into action, you will fail.

If you hold on too tight, you will lose your grip.

是以聖人無為故無敗；無執故無失。民之從事，常於幾成而敗之。
慎終如始，則無敗事，是以聖人欲不欲，不貴難得之貨；
學不學，復眾人之所過，以輔萬物之自然，而不敢為。

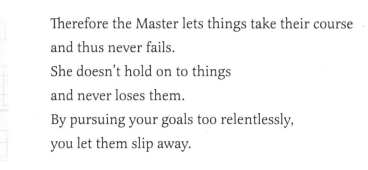

Therefore the Master lets things take their course
and thus never fails.
She doesn't hold on to things
and never loses them.
By pursuing your goals too relentlessly,
you let them slip away.

If you are as concerned about the outcome
as you are about the beginning,
then it is hard to do things wrong.
The Master seeks no possessions.
She learns by unlearning,
thus she is able to understand all things.
This gives her the ability to help all of creation.

65

古之善為道者，
非以明民，
將以愚之。
民之難治，
以其智多。
故以智治國，
國之賊；
不以智治國，
國之福。
知此兩者亦稽式。
常知稽式，
是謂玄德。
玄德深矣，
遠矣，與物反矣，
然後乃至大順。

The ancient Masters
who understood the way of the Tao,
did not educate people, but made them forget.

Smart people are difficult to guide,
because they think they are too clever.
To use cleverness to rule a country,
is to lead the country to ruin.
To avoid cleverness in ruling a country,
is to lead the country to prosperity.

Knowing the two alternatives is a pattern.
Remaining aware of the pattern is a virtue.
This dark and mysterious virtue is profound.
It is opposite our natural inclination,
but leads to harmony with the heavens.

**66**

江海所以能為百谷王者，以其善下之，故能為百谷王。
是以聖人欲上民，必以言下之；欲先民，必以身後之。
是以聖人處上而民不重，處前而民不害。
是以天下樂推而不厭。以其不爭，故天下莫能與之爭。

Rivers and seas are rulers
of the streams of hundreds of valleys
because of the power of their low position.

If you want to be the ruler of people,
you must speak to them like you are their servant.
If you want to lead other people,
you must put their interests ahead of your own.

The people will not feel burdened,
if a wise person is in a position of power.
The people will not feel like they are being manipulated,
if a wise person is in front as their leader.
The whole world will ask for her guidance,
and will never get tired of her.
Because she does not like to compete,
no one can compete with the things she accomplishes.

天下皆謂我道大，似不肖。夫唯大，故似不肖。
若肖久矣。其細也夫！我有三寶，持而保之。
一曰慈，二曰儉，三曰不敢為天下先。
慈故能勇；儉故能廣；不敢為天下先，故能成器長。
今舍慈且勇；舍儉且廣；舍後且先；死矣！
夫慈以戰則勝，以守則固。天將救之，以慈衛之。

The world talks about honouring the Tao,

but you can't tell it from their actions.

Because it is thought of as great,

the world makes light of it.

It seems too easy for anyone to use.

There are three jewels that I cherish:

compassion, moderation, and humility.

With compassion, you will be able to be brave,

With moderation, you will be able to give to others,

With humility, you will be able to become a great leader.

To abandon compassion while seeking to be brave,

or abandoning moderation while being benevolent,

or abandoning humility while seeking to lead

will only lead to greater trouble.

The compassionate warrior will be the winner,

and if compassion is your defence you will be secure.

Compassion is the protector of Heaven's salvation.

**68**

善為士者，不武；善戰者，不怒；善勝敵者，
不與；善用人者，為之下。是謂不爭之德，
是謂用人之力，是謂配天古之極。

The best warriors
do not use violence.
The best generals
do not destroy indiscriminately.
The best tacticians
try to avoid confrontation.
The best leaders
become servants of their people.

This is called the virtue of non-competition.
This is called the power to manage others.
This is called attaining harmony with the heavens.

用兵有言：吾不敢為主，
而為客；不敢進寸，
而退尺。是謂行無行；
攘無臂；扔無敵；執無兵。
禍莫大於輕敵，
輕敵幾喪吾寶。
故抗兵相加，哀者勝矣。

There is an old saying:
'It is better to become passive
in order to see what will happen.
It is better to retreat a foot
than to advance only an inch.'

This is called
being flexible while advancing,
pushing back without using force,
and destroying the enemy without engaging him.

There is no greater disaster
than underestimating your enemy.
Underestimating your enemy
means losing your greatest assets.
When equal forces meet in battle,
victory will go to the one
that enters with the greatest sorrow.

**70**

吾言甚易知，甚易行。
天下莫能知，莫能行。
言有宗，事有君。
夫唯無知，是以不我知。
知我者希，則我者貴。
是以聖人被褐懷玉。

My words are easy to understand
and easier to put into practice.
Yet no one in the world seems to understand them,
nor are they able to apply what I teach.

My teachings come from the ancients,
the things I do are done for a reason.

Because you do not know me,
you are not able to understand my teachings.
Because those who know me are few,
my teachings become even more precious.

知不知上；不知知病。
夫唯病病，是以不病。
聖人不病，以其病病，
是以不病。

Knowing you don't know is wholeness.
Thinking you know is a disease.
Only by recognizing that you have an illness
can you move to seek a cure.

The Master is whole because
she sees her illnesses and treats them,
and thus is able to remain whole.

72

民不畏威，則大威至。
無狎其所居，無厭其所生。
夫唯不厭，是以不厭。
是以聖人自知不自見；
自愛不自貴。故去彼取此。

When people become overly bold,
then disaster will soon arrive.

Do not meddle with people's livelihood;
by respecting them they will in turn respect you.

Therefore, the Master knows herself but is not arrogant.
She loves herself but also loves others.
This is how she is able to make appropriate choices.

**73**

勇於敢則殺，勇於
不敢則活。此兩
者，或利或害。
天之所惡，孰知其
故？是以聖人猶難
之。天之道，不爭
而善勝，不言而善
應，不召而自來，
繟然而善謀。天網
恢恢，疎而不失。

Being overbold and confident is deadly.
The wise use of caution will keep you alive.

One is the way to death,
and the other is the way to preserve your life.
Who can understand the workings of Heaven?

The Tao of the universe
does not compete, yet wins;
does not speak, yet responds;
does not command, yet is obeyed;
and does not act, but is good at directing.

The nets of Heaven are wide,
but nothing escapes its grasp.

民不畏死，奈何以死懼之？若使民常畏死，而為奇者，
吾得執而殺之，孰敢？常有司殺者殺。夫司殺者，
是大匠斲；夫代大匠斲者，希有不傷其手矣。

If you do not fear death,
then how can it intimidate you?
If you aren't afraid of dying,
there is nothing you cannot do.

Those who harm others
are like inexperienced boys
trying to take the place
of a great lumberjack.
Trying to fill his shoes
will only get them seriously hurt.

民之飢，以其上食稅之多，是以飢。
民之難治，以其上之有為，是以難治。
民之輕死，以其求生之厚，是以輕死。
夫唯無以生為者，是賢於貴生。

## 75

When people go hungry,
the government's taxes are too high.
When people become rebellious,
the government has become too intrusive.

When people begin to view death lightly,
wealthy people have too much
which causes others to starve.

Only those who do not cling to their life can save it.

**76**

人之生也柔弱，其死也堅強。
萬物草木之生也柔脆，其死也枯槁。
故堅強者死之徒，柔弱者生之徒。
是以兵強則不勝，木強則共。
強大處下，柔弱處上。

The living are soft and yielding;
the dead are rigid and stiff.
Living plants are flexible and tender;
the dead are brittle and dry.

Those who are stiff and rigid
are the disciples of death.
Those who are soft and yielding
are the disciples of life.

The rigid and stiff will be broken.
The soft and yielding will overcome.

天之道，
其猶張弓與？
高者抑之，
下者舉之；
有餘者損之，
不足者補之。
天之道，
損有餘而補不足。
人之道，則不然，
損不足以奉有餘。
孰能有餘以奉天下，
唯有道者。
是以聖人為而不恃，
功成而不處，
其不欲見賢。

The Tao of Heaven works in the world
like the drawing of a bow.
The top is bent downward;
the bottom is bent up.
The excess is taken from,
and the deficient is given to.

The Tao works to use the excess,
and gives to that which is depleted.
The way of people is to take from the depleted,
and give to those who already have an excess.

Who is able to give to the needy from their excess?
Only someone who is following the way of the Tao.

This is why the Master gives
expecting nothing in return.
She does not dwell on her past accomplishments,
and does not glory in any praise.

天下莫柔弱於水，而攻堅強者莫之能勝，其無以易之。弱之勝強，
柔之勝剛，天下莫不知，莫能行。是以聖人云：受國之垢，
是謂社稷主；受國不祥，是謂天下王。正言若反。

**78**

Water is the softest and most yielding substance.
Yet nothing is better than water,
for overcoming the hard and rigid,
because nothing can compete with it.

Everyone knows that the soft and yielding
overcomes the rigid and hard,
but few can put this knowledge into practice.

Therefore the Master says:
'Only he who is the lowest servant of the kingdom,
is worthy of becoming its ruler.
He who is willing to tackle the most unpleasant tasks,
is the best ruler in the world.'

True sayings seem contradictory.

202 ● TAO TE CHING

和大怨，必有餘怨；安可以為善？
是以聖人執左契，而不責於人。
有德司契，無德司徹。
天道無親，常與善人。

Difficulties remain, even after solving a problem.
How then can we consider that as good?

Therefore the Master
does what she knows is right,
and makes no demands of others.
A virtuous person will do the right thing,
and persons with no virtue will take advantage of others.

The Tao does not choose sides,
the good person receives from the Tao
because she is on its side.

小國寡民。使有什伯之器而不用；使民重死而不遠徙。
雖有舟輿，無所乘之，雖有甲兵，無所陳之。
使民復結繩而用之，甘其食，美其服，安其居，樂其俗。
鄰國相望，雞犬之聲相聞，民至老死，不相往來。

## 80

Small countries with few people are best.
Give them all of the things they want,
and they will see that they do not need them.
Teach them that death is a serious thing,
and to be content to never leave their homes.
Even though they have plenty
of horses, wagons and boats,
they won't feel that they need to use them.
Even if they have weapons and shields,
they will keep them out of sight.
Let people enjoy the simple technologies,
let them enjoy their food,
let them make their own clothes,
let them be content with their own homes,
and delight in the customs that they cherish.
Although the next country is close enough
that they can hear their roosters crowing and
    dogs barking,
they are content never to visit each other
all of the days of their life.

信言不美，美言不信。善者不辯，辯者不善。知者不博，博者不知。聖人不積，既以為人己愈有，既以與人己愈多。天之道，利而不害；聖人之道，為而不爭。

True words do not sound beautiful;
beautiful-sounding words are not true.
Wise men don't need to debate;
men who need to debate are not wise.

Wise men are not scholars,
and scholars are not wise.
The Master desires no possessions.
Since the things she does are for the people,
she has more than she needs.
The more she gives to others,
the more she has for herself.

The Tao of Heaven nourishes by not forcing.
The Tao of the Wise Person acts by not competing.

# Picture Credits

**Art Archive**
8, 18-19, 72-73

**Bridgeman Art Library**
2, 6, 7, 10, 11, 13, 22, 23, 24-25, 26-27, 32-33, 34-35, 38-39, 50-51, 58, 61, 66-67, 76-77, 82-83, 84-85, 106-107, 117, 138-139, 140, 144-145, 156-157, 165, 194-195

**Corbis**
12, 16-17, 20-21, 108-109, 152-153

**Getty**
30-31

**Metropolitan Museum of Art**
4-5, 36-37, 42-43, 46-47, 56, 57, 63, 64-65, 68, 70, 74-75, 86, 96-97, 99, 100-101, 102, 104-105, 110, 111, 112-113, 114-115, 119, 122-123, 124-125, 126-127, 128-129, 130, 132-133, 134, 136-137, 148, 150-151, 154-155, 158-159, 160-161, 162-163, 166-167, 168-169, 172, 174-175, 176, 179, 180-181, 182-183, 184-185, 186-187, 190-191, 192, 196-197, 200-201, 203, 204-205, 206

**NPM**
120-121

**Shutterstock**
52, 54

**Wikipedia Creative Commons**
1, 9, 14, 14-15, 28-29, 41, 44, 45, 48, 49, 53, 55, 78-79, 81, 88-89, 91, 92-93, 94, 142-143, 146-147, 170-171, 189, 198-199, 208